KEEP FIT *WITH YOUR* CAT

A Cat Owners Fitness Manual

by
Richard Porteus

POWERFRESH
Northampton. U.K.

Under License from
CCC Publications . Los Angeles . US

Published in the UK by
POWERFRESH Limited
3 Gray Street
Northampton
NN1 3QQ

Telephone 44 01604 30996
Facsimile 44 01604 21013

Under License from CCC publications
California, USA

Cover and interior illustration CCC Publications

Cover Graphics and Interior Layout Powerfresh

KEEP FIT WITH YOUR CAT.
ISBN 1 874125 30 9

Printed in the UK by Avalon Print Northampton.
        Powerfresh July 1994

INTRODUCTION

Why is a cat better then an exercise machine? Answer: An exercise machine keeps you in one place, but a cat takes you all over the house and the neighbourhood. It's true, you don't have to feed an exercise machine or set it in a litter box. But a cat doesn't tend to stick, squeak or wobble. Also no adjustment of the cat is necessary and one size fits all.

Of course, there are other exercise options available. You could exercise to a jazz workout video on a VCR if you like to dance on the spot while watching people sweating to music. Or, you could exercise on a tennis court hitting a ball over a net in such a way that it bounces and beats any attempts by your opponent to return it.

BEST BET: choose to exercise with your cat. No excess sweating, no tennis court. Most importantly - friendly, playful companionship is your reward as well as the conditioning of your entire body.

So, get fit with your cat!

THE EXERCISE : Rear End Push ups

1. BEND OVER WITH YOUR BODY,
    PLACING YOUR FOREARMS ON
    THE FLOOR, PALMS DOWN,
    STOMACH IN.

2. ROLL UP HIGH ON THE BALLS
    OF YOUR FEET AS YOU
    INHALE, LOWER YOUR HEELS
    AS YOU EXHALE.

    REPEAT 8 - 12 TIMES

THE APPLICATION : CHOOSING A CAT

THE EXERCISE : TOUCHING YOUR TOES

1. STAND UP AND LET YOUR BODY HANG DOWN FROM YOUR HIPS, WITH ARMS NOT QUITE TOUCHING THE FLOOR.

2. BOUNCE UP AND DOWN A FEW TIMES BREATHING SLOWLY AND DEEPLY.

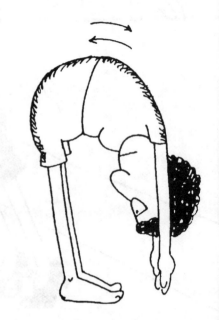

THE APPLICATION : TIDYING UP AFTER YOUR CAT

THE EXERCISE : UPWARD CLIMB

1. FACE THE WALL.

2. CLAW AT THE WALL WITH YOUR ARMS AND LEGS, PRETENDING THAT THE WALL IS A MOUNTAIN THAT MUST BE CLIMBED.

THE APPLICATION : DEMOUSING YOUR CAT

THE EXERCISE : BENT KNEE JUMPS

1. BEND YOUR KNEES.

2. JUMP AS HIGH AS YOU CAN WITH YOUR ARMS SPREAD OUT.

   REPEAT 5 TIMES

THE EXERCISE : ROCKING

1. SIT ON THE FLOOR

2. BEND YOUR KNEES.
   KEEP YOUR FEET APART.

3. ROCK BACK AND FORTH
   GENTLY.

   CONTINUE FOR ABOUT 30 SECONDS

THE APPLICATION: PLAYING WITH YOUR CAT

THE EXERCISE : LUNGES

1. STAND UP STRAIGHT, FEET TOGETHER, ARMS DOWN.

2. LUNGE FORWARD ON YOUR RIGHT LEG, BRINGING YOUR RIGHT ARM FORWARD AS YOU DO SO.

3. RETURN TO START POSITION.

   REPEAT 5 TIMES WITH EACH LEG

THE APPLICATION : FENCING WITH YOUR CAT

THE EXERCISE : KNEE PULL UPS

1. STAND UP AND HOLD ONTO A CHAIR WITH YOUR LEFT HAND FOR SUPPORT. BRING YOUR KNEE UP TO YOUR CHEST FOUR TIMES.

2. SWITCH TO YOUR OTHER LEG

3. TRY THE PULL UPS FAST - WITHOUT A CHAIR!

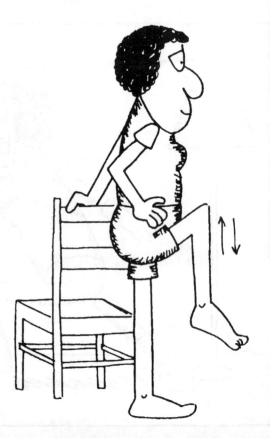

THE EXERCISE : REACH FOR THE SKY

1. IN A STANDING POSITION, RAISE BOTH YOUR ARMS ABOVE YOUR HEAD.

2. NOW ALTERNATE, REACHING ONE HAND AT A TIME UP TOWARD THE SKY. REACH FROM YOUR WAIST.

   DO 8 - 12 REACHES

THE APPLICATION : VISITING THE VET

THE EXERCISE : BUTTERFLY

1. STAND WITH YOUR ARMS BY YOUR SIDE AND YOUR LEGS TOGETHER.

2. JUMP UP AS YOU SPREAD YOUR ARMS AND LEGS.

3. BRING YOUR ARMS DOWN AND YOUR LEGS TOGETHER BEFORE YOU REACH THE FLOOR.

REPEAT 5 - 6 TIMES

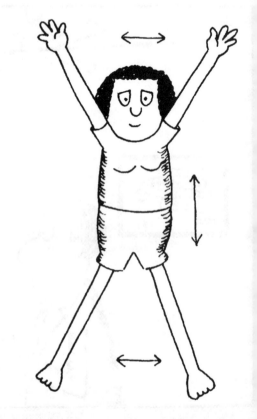

THE APPLICATION : HELPING YOUR CAT CROSS THE ROAD

THE EXERCISE : CRAB WALK

1. FROM A STANDING POSITION, BEND DOWN AND PLACE YOUR HANDS FLAT ON THE FLOOR. TRY TO KEEP LEGS STRAIGHT.

2. WALK FORWARD ON YOUR HANDS UNTIL YOUR BODY IS ALMOST PARALLEL WITH THE FLOOR.

3. PAUSE, THEN WALK BACKWARDS ON YOUR HANDS UNTIL THEY MEET YOUR FEET

REPEAT 4 TIMES

THE APPLICATION : PROTECTING YOUR CAT

THE EXERCISE : WALKING

1. AS YOU WALK, MAINTAIN
   UNBROKEN CONTACT WITH THE
   GROUND. THE REAR FOOT MUST
   NOT LEAVE THE GROUND BEFORE
   THE ADVANCING FOOT HAS MADE
   CONTACT. YOUR LEG MUST BE
   MOMENTARILY STRAIGHTENED
   WHILE A FOOT IS ON THE GROUND.

THE APPLICATION : EXERCISING YOUR CAT

THE EXERCISE : ARM LIFTS

1. KNEEL.

2. LIFT YOUR ARMS FROM A
   LOWER TO A HIGHER POSITION.

   REPEAT 8 - 10 TIMES

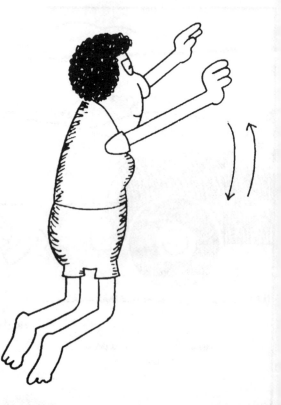

THE APPLICATION : BATHING YOUR CAT

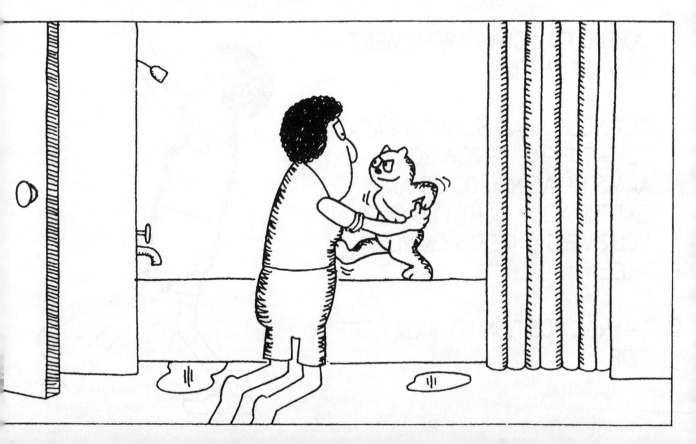

THE EXERCISE : ARM SWINGS

DO THE FOLLOWING MOVEMENT
TO FAST MUSIC :

1. TILT YOUR HEAD SLIGHTLY BACK
   TO THE RIGHT. THROW YOUR
   ARMS UP AS YOU DO SO AND
   EXTEND YOUR RIGHT LEG SO THAT
   YOUR WEIGHT RESTS ON YOUR
   HEEL.

2. CHANGE POSITION TO YOUR LEFT
   SIDE.

THE APPLICATION : DRYING YOUR CAT

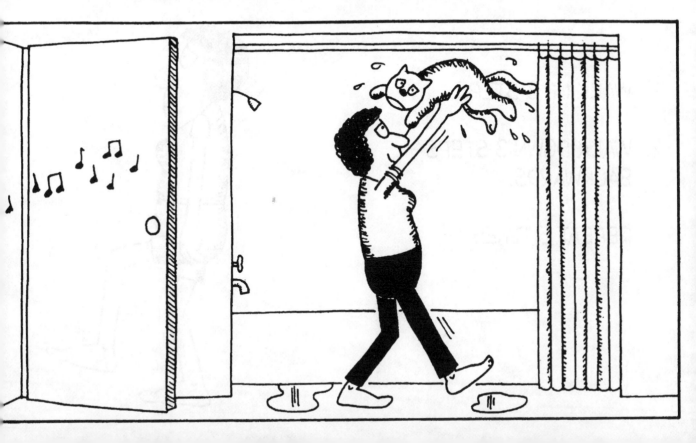

THE EXERCISE : STEP UPS

1. WALK UP 3 STEPS.

2. WALK DOWN 3 STEPS - BACKWARDS.

   REPEAT 5 TIMES

THE APPLICATION: TAKING YOUR CAT TO KENNELS

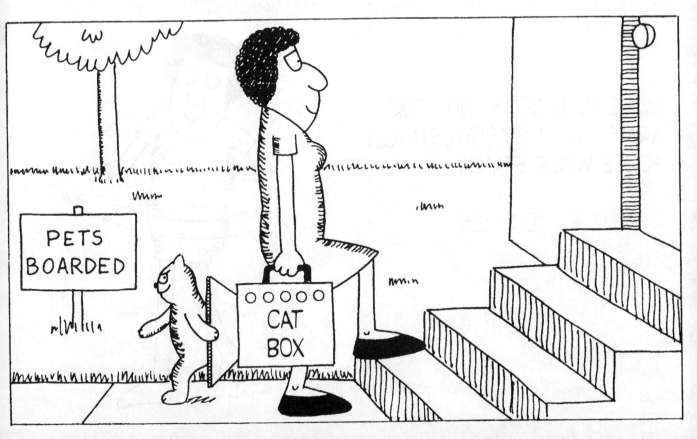

THE EXERCISE : BODY TWISTS

MOVE YOUR BODY AND YOUR
ARMS WITH A SMOOTH STEADY
FORCE WHILE STANDING IN PLACE.

REPEAT 8 - 10 TIMES.

THE APPLICATION : DISTRACTING YOUR CAT

THE EXERCISE : CROUCHING

1. GET DOWN ON YOUR KNEES AND ELBOWS.

2. MOVE FORWARD 5 FEET THEN BACKWARD 5 FEET.

   REPEAT 6 TIMES

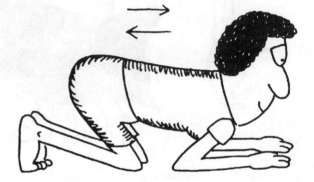

THE APPLICATION : COAXING YOUR CAT

THE EXERCISE : SWING THROUGH

1. STAND UP AND SWING ONE ARM IN FRONT OF YOU.

2. AT THE SAME TIME SWING ONE LEG OUT.

3. ALTERNATE AN ARM AND A LEG.

   REPEAT 6 TIMES.

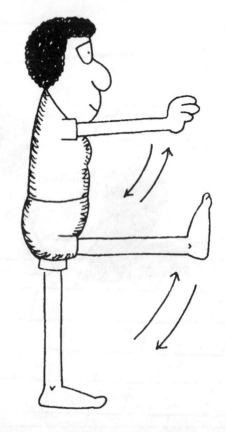

THE APPLICATION : REMOVING YOUR CAT

THE EXERCISE : CLAP AND JUMP

CLAP YOUR HANDS WHILE
JUMPING UP AND DOWN.

REPEAT FOR ONE MINUTE.

THE APPLICATION : SHOOING YOUR CAT

THE EXERCISE : ROCKING HORSE

1. LIE ON YOUR STOMACH, BEND YOUR KNEES, AND HOLD YOUR ANKLES.

2. PULL YOUR FEET AWAY FROM YOUR BODY, SO THAT YOUR KNEES ARE LIFTED OFF THE FLOOR. HOLD FOR A COUNT OF 3.

3. RETURN TO STARTING POSITION.

   DO 5 TIMES

THE APPLICATION : TEACHING YOUR CAT TO SKYDIVE

THE EXERCISE : Chorus Line Kicks

1. PLAY FAST MUSIC.

2. EXTEND YOUR ARMS AND KICK YOUR RIGHT LEG UP AND DOWN TO THE MUSIC TWO OR THREE TIMES.

3. ALTERNATE WITH YOUR LEFT LEG.

   REPEAT UNTIL THE MUSIC STOPS.

THE EXERCISE : FOOT SHAKING

1. BEND YOUR KNEES
   TOWARDS YOUR CHEST
   AND LIFT YOUR LEGS IN
   THE AIR, KEEPING YOUR
   KNEES SLIGHTLY BENT.

2. SHAKE YOUR FEET AND
   LEGS FORCEFULLY ABOUT
   20-30 SECONDS

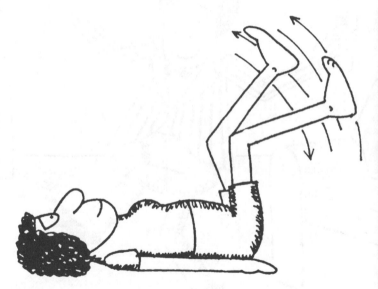

THE EXERCISE : ROLL OVERS

1. LIE DOWN ON YOUR BACK.

2. RAISE YOUR FOREARMS AND
   LEGS STRAIGHT UP.

3. SLOWLY ROLL ONTO YOUR RIGHT
   SIDE, THEN ONTO YOUR
   LEFT SIDE.

   REPEAT 8 TIMES

THE EXERCISE : CATWALKING

WALK BY PLACING
ONE FOOT DIRECTLY
IN FRONT OF THE OTHER.

THE APPLICATION : BONDING WITH YOUR CAT

THE EXERCISE : RUNNING

MOVE ON FOOT
AT A PACE FASTER
THAN A WALK AND
IN SUCH A WAY THAT
BOTH FEET LEAVE
THE GROUND AT EACH
STRIDE.

THE APPLICATION : PURSUING YOUR CAT

THE EXERCISE : BODY BENDS

1. FROM A STANDING POSITION, BEND YOUR KNEES. BEND OVER AND PLACE YOUR PALMS ON YOUR KNEES SO YOU WON'T LOSE BALANCE.

2. RETURN TO STANDING POSITION.

REPEAT 8 - 12 TIMES

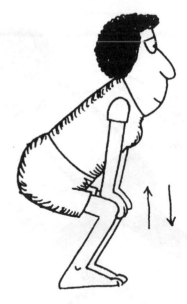

THE APPLICATION : CALLING YOUR CAT

THE EXERCISE : BENT KNEE STRETCH

1. STAND UP AND REACH OUT WITH BOTH HANDS.

2. BEND YOUR KNEES SLOWLY AND BRING YOUR BOTTOM DOWN TO YOUR HEELS.

3. STAND UP SLOWLY

THE EXERCISE : CRUNCHES

1. LIE ON THE FLOOR ON YOUR BACK.

2. CLASP YOUR HANDS BEHIND YOUR HEAD. PULL UP YOUR KNEES TO YOUR CHEST, BRINGING YOUR HEAD AND ELBOWS TO MEET YOUR KNEES AS YOU INHALE.

3. STRAIGHTEN YOUR LEGS AS YOU LOWER YOUR HEAD, THEN OPEN YOUR ELBOWS AS YOU EXHALE.

REPEAT 12 TIMES.

THE EXERCISE : TOSSING AND TURNING

WHILE LYING DOWN
THROW YOURSELF
FROM SIDE TO SIDE.

REPEAT 6 TIMES.

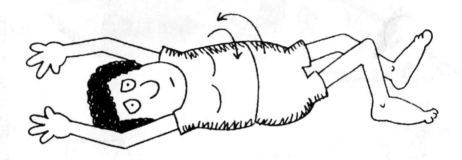

APPLICATION : REACTING TO YOUR INSOMNIAC CAT

THE EXERCISE : THE PELVIC TOSS

1. LIE DOWN ON YOUR BACK WITH YOUR HANDS UNDER YOUR HIPS.

2. RAISE YOUR LEGS AND TORSO TOWARDS THE SKY. PUSH YOUR LEGS BEYOND YOUR HEAD.

   HOLD THIS POSITION FOR TWO MINUTES OR SO.

THE APPLICATION : SHARING YOUR BED

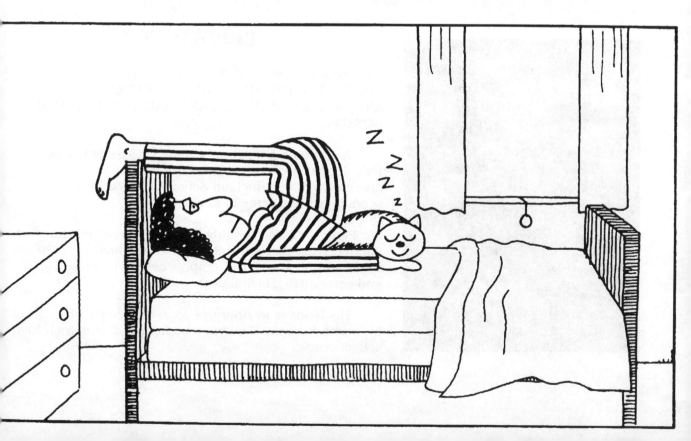

BIOGRAPHY

Richard Porteus is the author and illustrator of CREATIVE MATH, THINKING CREATIVELY, ARTS AND CRAFTS YOU CAN MAKE, and DISCOVER BOSTON.

A graduate of Fitchburg State College with a master's degree in education from Boston University, he attended the New England School of Art in Boston after serving with the army in Korea.

Mr. Porteus retired recently after 37 years of teaching art (kindergarten through college). During those years he freelanced as a muralist, graphic designer, charicaturist and cartoonist. He still does.

His home is in Braintree Massachusetts, where he lives with his wife, Carolyn, who he met during their high school years.

OTHER PUBLICATIONS BY
POWERFRESH

Crinkled n' Wrinkled	£ 2.99
Driven Crazy	£ 2.99
Oh No it's Xmas Again	£ 2.99
It's a Boy	£ 2.99
It's a Girl	£ 2.99
Now We Are 40	£ 2.99
Funny Side of 40 Him	£ 2.99
Funny Side of 40 Her	£ 2.99
Funny Side of 50 Him	£ 2.99
Funny Side of 50 Her	£ 2.99
Funny Side of Golf	£ 2.99
Funny Side of 60's	£ 2.99
Funny Side of Sex	£ 2.99
Get Stuffed	£ 2.99
Gerry's Atric Gag Book	£ 2.99

MORE PUBLICATIONS BY
POWERFRESH

Bastard's Golf	£ 2.99
Bastard's Sport	£ 2.99
Bastard's Life	£ 2.99
Bastard's Sex	£ 2.99
Bastard's Business	£ 2.99
Wimp's Sex	£ 2.99
Malcom	£ 2.99